A Simple Introduction To

DATA SCIENCE

A Simple Introduction To

DATA SCIENCE

by

Noreen Burlingame & Lars Nielsen

2012
New Street Communications, LLC
Wickford, RI

newstreetcommunications.com

Note: *A Brief Introduction to Data Science* was previously
published in a much different form as *The Little Book of Data
Science* by Noreen Burlingame. The book has been thoroughly
revised, updated and expanded by Lars Nielsen for this newly
titled edition.

Published November 2012
New Street Communications, LLC
Wickford, Rhode Island

newstreetcommunications.com

Contents

Data Science Summarized/1

What is Big Data/7

Hadoop/13

Data Management/22

Data Cleaning/26

Data Modeling for Unstructured Data/31

Predictive Analysis/38

Creativity and Intuition (or Posing the Right
Question, at the Right Time, for the Right Data)/42

Data Visualization (or Telling the Story)/50

Cassandra/55

Academic Programs/59

1

Data Science Summarized

Computers are like Old Testament Gods. Lots of rules and no mercy.

- Joseph Campbell -

In May of 2011, consulting firm McKinsey and Company issued a report in which it predicted organizations being deluged with data in the years to come. They also predicted that a range of major industries – including health care, the public sector, retail, and manufacturing – will benefit greatly from analyzing this rapidly growing pile of information generally referred to as "Big Data." (Please see chapter two for a detailed breakdown of Big Data and its various components.)

"Collecting and analyzing transactional data will give organizations more insight into their customers' preferences," writes Joab Jackson of IDG News. "It can be used to better inform the creation of products and services, and allow organizations to remedy emerging problems more quickly."

"The use of big data will become a key basis of competition and growth for individual firms," the McKinsey report concludes. "The use of big data will underpin new waves of productivity growth and consumer surplus."

The field of "Data Science" lies at the core of this revolution.

Wikibon and IDC both promise a Big Data market in 2015 of between $16.9 billion (IDC) to $32.1 billion (Wikibon). Recently, none other than Tim O'Reilly declared that 'data science is the new black.'"

Enter the "data scientists" – an elite and specialized class of highly-compensated data cleaning, analysis, and visualization experts. "Data scientists will be a special breed," says Press, "the only people with the experience and expertise to wrestle with the messy explosion of both digital (and dirty) data and big data tools. Data Science will become a specialized, in-house function, similar to today's Accounting, Legal, and IT departments. Leading universities will establish stand-alone Data Science departments, conferring data science degrees,

Bachelor's to Ph.D. ... Data scientists will be either academics, independent consultants, or members of the corporate data science function, where they will rise to the title of CDO (understood in leading organizations as Chief Decision Officer and by laggards as Chief Data Officer)."

This high-priesthood of data scientists will be much in demand, and highly-compensated. McKinsey and Company forecasts a major shortage of data science professionals over the coming years. McKinsey analysts predict that in 2018, for example, the USA will be short 1.5 million workers with the necessary deep analytical skill to mine Big Data for actionable information on which to base effective business decisions – not to mention also being short approx. 190,000 workers with the necessary data processing skills. According to Forrester research analyst James Kobielus: "[Organizations will] have to ... hire statistical modelers, text mining professionals, people who specialize in sentiment analysis." These same people must also be skilled in developing adaptive software models, data cleaning and mining, and related tasks.

As suggested above, Data Science is a multidisciplinary endeavor combining a range of skills in a variety of fields, together with *a strong talent for creative, intuitive thinking: the envisioning of new and useful data sets..*

"I think of Data Science as a flag that was planted at the intersection of several different disciplines that have not always existed in the same place," says Hilary Mason, chief data scientist at bitly. "Statistics, computer science, domain expertise, and what I usually call 'hacking,' though I don't mean the 'evil' kind of hacking. I mean the ability to take all those statistics and computer science, mash them together and actually make something work."

Mason divides data science into two equally important functions. One half is analytics or, as she describes it, "counting things." The other half is the invention of new techniques that can draw insights from data that were not possible before. "Data Science is the combination of analytics and the development of new algorithms. You may have to invent something, but it's okay if you can answer a question just by counting. The key is making the effort to ask the questions. ... If I ask a question like 'how many clicks did this link get?' which is something we look at all the time, that's not a data science question. It's an analytics question. If I ask a question like, 'based on the previous history of links on this publisher's site, can I predict how many people from France will read this in the next three hours?,' that's more of a Data Science question."

"[Data Science] absolutely gives us a competitive advantage if we can better understand what people care about and better use the data we have to create more relevant experiences," says Aaron Batalion, chief technology officer for online shopping service LivingSocial, which uses technologies such as the Apache Hadoop data processing platform (to be discussed in a later chapter) to mine insights about customer preferences. "The days are over when you build a product once and it just works," Batalion comments. "You have to take ideas, test them, iterate them, [and] use data and analytics to understand what works and what doesn't in order to be successful. And that's how we use our big data infrastructure."

Not only LivingSocial, but also such organizations as Google, Amazon, Yahoo, Facebook and Twitter have been on the cutting edge of leveraging the new discipline of Data Science to make the most of their growing piles of user information.

But Data Science remains a science for which tools are still being invented – a science in a state of flux. "There are vexing problems slowing the growth and the practical implementation of big data technologies," writes Mike Driscoll. "For the technologies to succeed at scale, there are several fundamental capabilities they should contain, including stream processing, palatalization, indexing, data evaluation environments and visualization." And all this evolution is ongoing.

In the following chapters, we shall explore the range of special skills/disciplines involved in the practice of Data Science. We shall also explore such key software tools as Hadoop and Cassandra, and take a glimpse at some of the most innovative and successful applications of Data Science to date. But first, we will define the essentials of that vital raw material upon which Data Science feeds: Big Data.

2

What is Big Data?

Part of the inhumanity of a computer is that, once it is competently programmed and working smoothly, it is completely honest.

- Isaac Asimov -

"You can't have a conversation in today's business technology world without touching on the topic of Big Data," says *NetworkWorld's* Michael Friedenberg. "Simply put, it's about data sets so large – in volume, velocity and variety – that they're impossible to manage with conventional database tools. In 2011, our global output of data was estimated at 1.8 zettabytes (each zettabyte equals 1 billion terabytes). Even more staggering is the widely quoted estimate that 90 percent of the data in the world was created within the past two years."

Friedenberg continues: "Behind this explosive growth in data, of course, is the world of unstructured data. At [the 2011] HP Discover Conference, Mike Lynch, executive vice president of information management and CEO of Autonomy, talked about the huge spike in the generation of unstructured data. He said the IT world is moving away from structured, machine-friendly information (managed in rows and columns) and toward the more human-friendly, unstructured data that originates from sources as varied as e-mail and social media and that includes not just words and numbers but also video, audio and images."

"Big Data means extremely scalable analytics," Forrester Research analyst James Kobielus told *Information Age* in October of 2011. "It means analyzing petabytes of structured and unstructured data at high velocity. That's what everybody's talking about."

As a catch-all term, "Big Data" is pretty nebulous. As *ZDNet's* Dan Kusnetzky notes: "If one sits through the presentations from ten suppliers of technology, fifteen or so different definitions are likely to come forward. Each definition, of course, tends to support the need for that supplier's products and services. Imagine that."

Industry politics aside, here's an unbiased definition of this complex field:

Every day of the week, we create 2.5 quintillion bytes of data. This data comes from everywhere: from sensors used to gather climate information, posts to social media sites, digital pictures and videos posted online, transaction records of online purchases, and from cell phone GPS signals – to name a few. In the 11 years between 2009 and 2020, the size of the "Digital Universe" will increase 44 fold. That's a 41% increase in capacity every year. In addition, only 5% of this data being created is structured and the remaining 95% is largely unstructured, or at best semi-structured. This is Big Data.

Per a recent analysis from IBM, Big Data Big comprises three dimensions: Variety, Velocity and Volume.

re: **Variety** – Big Data extends well beyond structured data, including unstructured data of all varieties: text, audio, video, click streams, log files and more.

re: **Velocity** – Frequently time-sensitive, Big Data *must be used simultaneously* with its stream in to the enterprise in order to maximize its value.

re: **Volume** – Big Data comes in one size: enormous. By definition, enterprises are awash with it, easily amassing terabytes and even petabytes of information. This volume presents the most immediate hurdle for conventional IT structures. It calls for scalable storage, and a distributed approach to querying. Many companies currently hold large amounts of archived data, but not the tools to process it.

(Note: To these three "V's", IBM's To this, IBM's Michael Schroeck adds **Veracity**. In other words, a firm's imperative to screen out spam and other data that is not useful for making business decisions.)

Per Edd Dumbill (and no, that is not a typo), program chair for the O'Reilly Strata Conference and the O'Reilly Open Source Convention, Big Data "is data that exceeds the processing capacity of conventional database systems. The data is too big, moves too fast, or doesn't fit the strictures of your database architectures. To gain value from this data, you must choose an alternative way to process it."

Dumbill continues: "The hot IT buzzword ... *Big Data* has become viable as cost-effective approaches have emerged to tame the volume, velocity and variability of massive data. Within this data lie valuable patterns and information, previously hidden because of the amount of work required to extract them. To leading corporations, such as Walmart or Google, this power has been in reach for some time, but at fantastic cost. Today's commodity hardware, cloud architectures and open source software bring Big Data processing into the reach of the less well-resourced. Big Data processing is eminently feasible for even the small garage startups, who can cheaply rent server time in the cloud."

Dumbill further explains that the value of Big Data falls into two categories: analytical use, and enabling new products. "Big Data analytics can reveal insights hidden previously by data too costly to process, such as peer influence among customers, revealed by analyzing shoppers' transactions, social and geographical data. Being able to process every item of data in reasonable time removes the troublesome need for sampling and promotes an investigative approach to data, in contrast to the somewhat static nature of running predetermined reports."

Overall, Big Data is – in its raw form – utter chaos. Approximately 80% of the effort involved in dealing with this largely-unstructured data is simply cleaning it up. Per Pete Warden in his *Big Data*

Glossary: "I probably spend more time turning messy source data into something usable than I do on the rest of the data analysis process combined."

The Data Scientist takes the "chaos" of "messy source data" and finds within this morass the pure gold of actionable market information.

Data Scientist =

Engineer +

Statistician + Analyst +

Hacker =

One **Totally Awesome** Nurd

3

Hadoop

That's what's cool about working with computers. They don't argue, they remember everything, and they don't drink all your beer.

- Paul Leary -

High performance data analysis is a required competitive component, providing valuable insight into the behavior of customers, market trends, scientific data, business partners, and internal users. Explosive growth in the amount of data businesses must track has challenged legacy database platforms. New unstructured, text-centric, data sources, such as feeds from Facebook and Twitter do not fit into the structured data model. These unstructured datasets tend to be very big and difficult to work with. *They demand distributed (aka parallelized) processing.*

Hadoop, an open source software product, has emerged as the preferred solution for Big Data analytics. Because of its scalability, flexibility, and low cost, it has become the default choice for Web giants that are dealing with large-scale clickstream analysis and ad targeting scenarios. For these reasons and more, many industries who have been struggling with the limitations of traditional database platforms are now deploying Hadoop solutions in their data centers. (These industries are also looking for economy. According to some recent research from Infineta Systems, a WAN optimization startup, traditional data storage runs $5 per gigabyte, but storing the same data costs about 25 cents per gigabyte using Hadoop.)

Businesses are finding they need faster insight and deeper analysis of their data – slow performance equates to lost revenue. Hadoop – available in customized, proprietary versions from a range of vendors – provides a solid answer to this dilemma.

Hadoop is a free, Java-based programming framework that supports the processing of large data sets in a distributed computing environment. It is part of the Apache project sponsored by the Apache Software Foundation.

Hadoop was originally conceived on the basis of Google's *MapReduce*, in which an application is broken down into numerous small parts. Any of these parts (also called fragments or blocks) can be run on any node in the cluster. Hadoop makes it possible to run applications on systems with thousands of nodes involving thousands of terabytes.

A distributed file system (DFS) facilitates rapid data transfer rates among nodes and allows the system to continue operating uninterrupted in case of a node failure. The risk of catastrophic system failure is low, even if a significant number of nodes become inoperative.

The Hadoop framework is used by major players including Google, Yahoo and IBM, largely for applications involving search engines and advertising. The preferred operating systems are Windows and Linux but Hadoop can also work with BSD and OS X. (A bit of trivia: the name *Hadoop* was inspired by the name of a stuffed toy elephant belonging to a child of the framework's creator, Doug Cutting.)

Hadoop lies, invisibly, at the heart of many Internet services accessed daily by millions users around the world.

"Facebook uses Hadoop ... extensively to process large data sets," says Ashish Thusoo, Engineering Manager at Facebook. "This infrastructure is used for a variety of different jobs – including adhoc analysis, reporting, index generation and many others. We have one of the largest clusters with a total storage disk capacity of more than 20PB and with more than 23000 cores. We also use Hadoop and Scribe for log collection, bringing in more than 50TB of raw data per day. Hadoop has helped us scale with these tremendous data volumes."

"Hadoop is a key ingredient in allowing LinkedIn to build many of our most computationally difficult features, allowing us to harness our incredible data about the professional world for our users," comments Jay Kreps, LinkedIn's Principal Engineer.

Let's not forget Twitter. "Twitter's rapid growth means our users are generating more and more data each day. Hadoop enables us to store, process, and derive insights from our data in ways that wouldn't otherwise be possible. We are excited about the rate of progress that Hadoop is achieving, and will continue our contributions to its thriving open source community," notes Kevin Weil, Twitter's Analytics Lead.

Then we have eBay. During 2010, eBay erected a Hadoop cluster spanning 530 servers. By December of 2011, the cluster was five times that large, helping with everything from analyzing inventory data to building customer profiles using real-time online behavior. "We got tremendous value – tremendous value – out of it, so we've expanded to 2,500 nodes," says Bob Page, eBay's vice president of analytics. "Hadoop is an amazing technology stack. We now depend on it to run eBay."

*

"Hadoop has been called the next-generation platform for data processing because it offers low cost and the ultimate in scalability. But Hadoop is still immature and will need serious work by the community ... " writes *InformationWeek's* Doug Henschen. "Hadoop is at the center of this decade's Big Data revolution. This Java-based framework is actually a collection of software and subprojects for distributed processing of huge volumes of data. The core approach is MapReduce, a technique used to boil down tens or even hundreds of terabytes of Internet clickstream data, log-file data, network traffic streams, or masses of text from social network feeds."

Henschen continues: "The clearest sign that Hadoop is headed mainstream is that fact that it was embraced by five major database and data management vendors in 2011, with EMC, IBM, Informatica, Microsoft, and Oracle all throwing their hats into the Hadoop ring. IBM and EMC released their own distributions last year, the latter in partnership with MapR. Microsoft and Oracle have partnered with Hortonworks and Cloudera, respectively. Both EMC and Oracle have delivered purpose-built appliances that are ready to run Hadoop. Informatica has extended its data-integration platform to support Hadoop, and it's also bringing its parsing and data-transformation code directly into the environment."

Still, says Henschen, Hadoop remains "downright crude compared to SQL [Structured Query Language, traditionally used to parse structured data]. Pioneers, most of whom started working on the framework at Internet giants such as Yahoo, have already put at least six years into developing Hadoop. But success has brought mainstream demand for stability, robust administrative and management capabilities, and the kind of rich functionality available in the SQL world. ... Data processing is one thing, but what most Hadoop users ultimately want to do is analyze the data. Enter Hadoop-specialized data access, business intelligence, and analytics vendors such as Datameer, Hadapt, and Karmasphere." (All three of these firms are to be discussed in later chapters.) (Note that the most popular approaches to parsing unstructured data are often referred to as NoSQL approaches/tools.)

*

Created from work done in Apache by Hortonworks, Yahoo! and the rest of the vibrant Apache community, Hadoop 0.23 – the first major update to Hadoop in three years – provides the critical foundation for the next wave of Apache Hadoop innovation. Featuring the next-generation MapReduce architecture, HDFS Federation and High Availability advancements, Hadoop 0.23 is at this writing [February 2012] available as individual project downloads from Apache.org. Apache Hadoop 0.23 is currently being actively tested and working its way towards a final, stable release later in 2012.

Additional Hadoop-related projects at Apache include: *Avro*, a data serialization system; *Cassandra*, a scalable multi-master database with no single points of failure; *Chukwa*, data collection system for managing large distributed systems; *HBase*, a scalable, distributed database that supports structured data storage for large tables; *Hive*, a data warehouse infrastructure that provides data summarization and ad hoc querying; *Mahout*, a scalable machine learning and data mining library; *Pig*, high-level data-flow language and execution framework for parallel computation; and *ZooKeeper*, a high-performance coordination service for distributed applications.

*

Note: Hadoop works best in collaboration with several specially designed tools. For example, Apache Pig is a high-level procedural language for querying large semi-structured data sets using Hadoop and the MapReduce Platform. Pig simplifies the use of Hadoop by allowing SQL-like queries to a distributed dataset. Then we have Apache Hbase. Use HBase when you need random, real-time read/write access to your Big Data. Hbase enables the hosting of very large tables – billions of rows X millions of columns – atop clusters of commodity hardware. HBase is an open-source, distributed, versioned, column-oriented store modeled after Google's *Bigtable*. Just as Bigtable leverages the distributed data storage provided by the Google File System, HBase provides Bigtable-like capabilities on top of Hadoop and HDFS.

We need to note two more items: Sqoop and Hive. Apache Sqoop is a tool designed for efficiently transferring bulk data between Apache Hadoop and structured datastores such as relational databases. Hadoop Hive, meanwhile, constitutes a robust data warehouse infrastructure providing powerful data summarization and ad hoc querying capabilities.

*

Note: Although clearly dominant, Hadoop – it should be mentioned – is not the only technology that sits under the Big Data umbrella. Other methodologies include columnar databases, which organize data by columns instead of rows and lend themselves to analytical data warehousing and compression.

4

Data Management

The function of good software is to make the complex appear to be simple.

- Grady Booch -

The right data management tools are key to making effective use of Big Data, turning its volume into a resource rather than a daunting mountain of unsorted bits and bytes. With the right data management techniques tools, Big Data can be divided relatively easily into manageable chunks.

Data analytics empower firms to dissect and study sets of data that matter most to them and their business goals.

Data capture is what's going on when firms get people to sign up to various things, asking for details at all opportunities and collecting consumer insight based on the accumulated data. However, none of it will make much sense unless the useful data sets have been directly identified.

Data management constitutes the systematic approach to dicing and slicing massive piles of data into logical, digestable portions.

The key step to effective data management is defining and adopting a comprehensive, systematic process for using Big Data. A major component of this is to centralize all information collected into a single place, rather than using disparate systems. Data quality software integration, together with data visualization tools, can help achieve this primary step: putting data into the right context, and in this way making it meaningful.

Once this is achieved, it becomes far easier to get the right data into the right hands. XMG analyst Jacky Garrido has commented in a *ZDnet* interview that enterprises must isolate the right sorts of data in order "to avoid getting buried under the humongous amount of information they generate through various outlets." Garrido compares Big Data to an ocean wave; companies must either ride on top of or be consumed by it."

Analytics for Big Data can involve any number of procedures, some deriving from the pure traditional sciences of uinivariate, bivariate, and multivariate analysis. Of course, univariate analysis refers to the study of single-variables, bivariate to the study of two, and multivariate to the application of univariate and bivariate procecures, plus other procedures, to multiple variables.

Stream Processing (aka, Real Time Analytic Processing – RTAP)

Remember how we said one key characteristic of Big Data is *velocity*? Yes, well that being the case, the Data Scientist is not so much interested in looking at a traditional "data set" as he or she is in studying "data streams." The Data Scientist must mine and analyze actionable data in real time using architectures that are capable of of processing streams of data *as they occur*. This is a major area of Big Data and Data Science where the best and most robust tools are still in the making. All in all, current database paradigms are not ideal for stream processing, although the algorithms already exist.

As Mike Driscoll notes: " … Calculating an average over a group of data can be done in a traditional batch process, but far more efficient algorithms exist for calculating a moving average of data as it arrives, incrementally, unit by unit. If you want to take a repository of data and perform almost any statistical analysis, that can be accomplished with open source products like R or commercial products like SAS. But if you want to create a set of streaming statistics, to which you incrementally add or remove a chunk of data as a moving average, the libraries either don't exist or are immature."

5

Data Cleaning

There are three kinds of lies: lies, damned lies, and statistics.

- George Bernard Shaw -

Data cleaning (sometimes also referred to as data cleansing or data scrubbing)is the act of detecting and either removing or correcting corrupt or inaccurate records from a record set, table, or database. Used mainly in cleansing databases, the process applies identifying incomplete, incorrect, inaccurate, irrelevant, etc. items of data and then replacing, modifying, or deleting this "dirty" information.

The next step after data cleaning is *data reduction*. This includes defining and extracting attributes, decreasing the dimensions of data, representing the problems to be solved, summarizing the data, and selecting portions of the data for analysis.

Generally, in order to be classified as "high-quality," data needs to pass a firm and exacting set of criteria. Those include:

Accuracy: an aggregated value over the criteria of integrity, consistency, and density

Integrity: an aggregated value over the criteria of completeness and validity

Completeness: achieved by correcting data containing anomalies

Validity: approximated by the amount of data satisfying integrity constraints

Consistency: concerns contradictions and syntactical anomalies

Uniformity: directly related to irregularities and in compliance with the set "unit of measure"

Density: the quotient of missing values in the data and the number of total values ought to be known

Sharon Machlis of *ComputerWorld* puts data cleaning into perspective: "Before you can analyze and visualize data, it often needs to be 'cleaned.' What does that mean? Perhaps some entries list 'New York City' while others say 'New York, NY' and you need to standardize them before you can see patterns.

There might be some records with misspellings or numerical data-entry errors." Such procedures as this constitute data cleaning.

Note: The need to analyze time-series or other forms of streaming (velocity) data poses unique data cleaning challenges. Examples of this class of data include economic time-series like stock prices, exchange rates, or unemployment figures, biomedical data sequences like electrocardiograms or electroencephalograms, or industrial process operating data sequences like temperatures, pressures or concentrations. Nevertheless fundamental principles of data cleaning apply just as much to these data sets as to any others.

Bruce Ratner, Ph.D. – of the highly-regarded *DM Stat-1 Consulting* – identifies ten fundamentals of data cleaning:

1. Check frequencies of continuous and categorical variables for unreasonable distributions.

2. Check frequencies of continuous and categorical variables for detection of unexpected values. For continuous variables, look into data "clumps" and "gaps."

3. Check for improbable values (e.g., a boy named Sue), and impossible values (e.g., age is 120 years young, and x/0).

4. Check the type for numeric variables: Decimal, integer, and date.

5. Check the meanings of misinformative values, e.g., "NA", the blank " ", the number "0", the letter "O", the dash "-", and the dot ". ".

6. Check for out-of-range data: Values "far out" from the "fences" of the data.

7. Check for outliers: Values "outside" the fences of the data.

8. Check for missing values, and the meanings of their coded values, e.g., the varied string of "9s", the number "0", the letter "O", the dash "-", and the dot ". ".

9. Check the logic of data, e.g., response rates cannot be 110%, and weigh contradictory values, along with conflict resolution rules, e.g., duplicate records of BR's DOB: 12/22/56 and 12/22/65.

10. Last but not least, check for the typos.

Ratner: "After the ten basic and analyst-specific checks are done, data cleaning is not completed until the *noise* in the data is eliminated. Noise is the idiosyncrasies of the data: The particulars, the "nooks and crannies" that are not part of the sought-after essence (e.g., predominant pattern) of the data with regard to the objective of the analysis/model. Ergo, the data particulars are lonely, not-really-belonging-to pieces of information that happen to be both in the population from which the data was drawn and in the data itself (what an example of a double-chance occurrence!) Paradoxically, as the analyst includes more and more of the prickly particulars in the analysis/model, the analysis/model becomes better and better, yet the analysis/model validation becomes worse and worse. Noise must be eliminated from the data."

6

Data Modeling for Unstructured Data

It is a capital mistake to theorize before one has data.

- Sherlock Holmes -

Data modeling is the analysis of data objects used in a business or other context and the identification of the relationships among these data objects. Another definition, this from Scott Ambler, Chief Methodologist for Agile and Lean within IBM Rational: "Data modeling is the act of exploring data-oriented structures. Like other modeling artifacts data models can be used for a variety of purposes, from high-level conceptual models to physical data models."

The sheer quantity and complexity of unstructured data opens up many new opportunities for the analyst and modeler. Imagine requirements such as: Show me consumer feedback on my product from all Website discussion groups for the last six months; Show me all photographs taken of the fountains in Rome from the summers of 2002 through 2007; Show me all contracts which contain a particular liability clause.

"So – what is a data model?" asks David Dichmann, Product Line Director for Design Tools at Sybase. "It is first and foremost a way to capture business language and information relationships that provide context to make it useful in decision making activities. It is then specialized into representations of storage paradigms, and ultimately, when appropriate, into detailed designs of physical systems where structures will be implemented to manage, store, move, transform and analyze data points. Today's data models are way beyond traditional logical/physical representations of database systems implementation. Today's data models are architectural drawings of the meaning and intent of information – simple, beautiful creations that drive the logic of applications, systems and technology and physical implementations of business information infrastructure."

Dichmann posits that the data model, if viewed as "an abstraction of the physical representation of the database structures," clearly declines in value in face of the schema-less [data] or the constantly changing schemas. "But, if it is the abstraction of the conceptual representation of the information, we see a rise in importance. The language of the business, and the context of data points, provide meaning to the analysis that we want to gain from these non-traditional systems. [We are on a journey] from points of data (records collected by recording all our 'transactions') to meaningful information (the collation, aggregation and analysis of points of data by applying context to data). With Big Data, we do not even consider the data points themselves but rather jump right to some trend analysis (aggregation of sorts). Interpretation comes from comparisons to a series of basis points to be used in decision making, taking data all the way to wisdom. The basis points themselves are context and can be modeled."

Some posit that with regard to big data, data modeling is a major obstacle to agile business intelligence (BI). The answer, according leading software analyst Barney Finucane.

"The need for data modeling depends upon the application. [Software] products that promise user friendly analysis without any data analysis are usually intended for a specific type of analysis that does not require any previously specified structure."

A good example of data that does not require modeling is what retailers gather about their customers. "This data comes in big flat tables with many columns, and the whole point to the analysis is to find unexpected patterns in this unstructured data. In this case adding a model is adding assumptions that may actually hinder the analysis process."

However, "some types of analyses only make sense with at least some modeling. Time intelligence is an example of a type of analysis that is supported by a data model. Also analyzing predefined internal structures such as cost accounts or complex sales channels is usually more convenient based on predefined structures. The alternative method of discovering the structures in the raw data may not be possible."

Finucane adds: "Planning is a common area of agile BI, and planning is rarely possible without predefined structures. It is no coincidence that the tools that promise analysis without data modeling do not offer planning features. Planning requires adding new data to an existing data set. In some cases, this includes adding new master data, for example when new products are being planned. Furthermore, there is often a good deal of custom business logic in a planning application that cannot be defined automatically. Most financial planning processes, and the analysis and simulation that goes along with them cannot be carried out on a simple table. In my view the new generation columnar databases are a welcome addition to agile BI. But I also think that their marketing is sometimes a little over the top when it comes to dismissing existing BI solution in this area."

Forrester Research analyst James Kobielus goes a step further: "Big data relies on solid data modeling. Statistical predictive models and test analytic models will be the core applications you will need to do big data."

But Brett Sheppard, executive director at Zettaforce and a former senior analyst at Gartner, disagrees. "Letting data speak for itself through analysis of entire data sets is eclipsing modeling from subsets. In the past, all too often what were once disregarded as 'outliers' on the far edges of a data model turned out to be the telltale signs of a micro-trend that became a major event. To enable this advanced analytics and integrate in real-time with operational processes, companies and public sector organizations are evolving their enterprise architectures to incorporate new tools and approaches."

Ultimately, it is important to remember re: data modeling for Big Data is that any given model is just a simplified representation of reality and can take many forms.

One of the best tools for the modeling of unstructured data is Apache Cassandra, this to be discussed at length in a subsequent chapter. The most important aspect of Cassandra and other such tools is that they allow the flexibility required to ensure data models are scaled in a way that is cost-effective with regard to unstructured Big Data, especially the application of multidimensional data models, vertical industry data models and customizable analytics problem algorithms.

In the final analysis, a data model for Big Data is useless without the human element: the skilled eye of the data scientist, discerning subtleties ('outliers') in data. "Data sparsity, non-linear interactions and the resultant model's quirks must be interpreted through the lens of domain expertise," writes Ben Gimpert of Altos Research. "All Big Data models are wrong but some are useful, to paraphrase the statistician George Box. A data scientist working in isolation could train a predictive model with perfect in-sample accuracy, but only an understanding of how the business will use the model lets [him or her] balance the crucial bias/variance trade-off. *Put more simply, applied business knowledge is how we can assume a model trained on historical data will do decently with situations we have never seen."*

The key to optimal data modeling is the talent to intuitively look for outliers in information characteristics ... to find what you don't recognize as valuable *until you find it.*

7

Predictive Analysis

It is tough to make predictions, especially about the future.

- Yogi Berra -

Tech journalist Jon Gertner has written: "It now seems possible that the [social] networks' millions of posts and status updates are adding up to something culturally and financially priceless." In a recent piece for *The New York Times*, Gertner cited to key examples:

1. HP Labs has developed an algorithm that analyzes Twitter messages about newly released films. The results are used to predict how well these films will perform at the box office long-term, and the algorithm has thus far out-performed (in terms of accuracy) a long-standing tool called the Hollywood Stock Exchange used for the same purpose.

2. A research team at Indiana University recently classified close to 10 million tweets into six "mood categories" (alertness, calmness, happiness, kindness, sureness, and vitality). The team leader, Johan Bollen, was actually surprised to find that the results "could predict changes in the Dow Jones Industrial Average." Bollen says he expected the mood on Twitter would be a *reflection* of up and down movements in the stock market. He never imagined it would be a precursor. But it is.

As Gertner writes: "Social scientists have begun looking more broadly at the aggregate value of social media." Thus the rise of predictive analysis as the key to extracting maximum business intelligence from this Big Data.

Predictive analysis gives organizations full investigative power to delve into any corner of data to discover otherwise obscure details behind specific performance outcomes. The main idea of predictive analysis is to use current and past data to predict future events. The goal of the statistical techniques used in predictive analysis is to determine market patterns, identify risks, and predict potential opportunities for growth. In addition, data relationships can be reordered to determine the most plausible outcome of possible solutions and patterns can be recognized that might have the power to alter the outcome of a probable event.

Eric Robson, leader of the Data Mining and Social Networks Analysis Group at the TSSG, a part of Ireland's Waterford Institute of Technology, explains: "For instance, a large supermarket has many thousands of customers and many thousands of products to sell. Usually each customer is tracked via their charge card ... and we are able to see return visits. On day one, a customer might buy bread and some butter. On day three, they buy some more bread but it might not be until day fourteen that they need to buy some more butter. From this simple example we can see how a trend or a purchasing pattern can be determined." *This*, then, is predictive analysis.

Robson continues: "In social network predictive analytics people are constantly passing messages to each other. From a marketing perspective we can look at who we should be targeting to send our viral message out to for further [propagation.] Who are the biggest distributors of content? It may not necessarily be commercial entities. It could be; bloggers, people with very active Facebook accounts, people with very active Twitter accounts. In terms of product, we can start identifying who are the key influencers. Say, IOracle Advanced Analytics Option wanted to sell something like running shoes and this guy is a marathon runner and blogs about them. If we know that people listen to him then the running shoe manufacturer can start targeting this guy. 'Here's a free pair of running shoes. Tell us what you think of them.' More importantly, 'Tell the world what you think of them.'"

In the past, marketers would use relatively small numbers to extrapolate a larger result. With social media, they can look at thousands or millions of opinions and come to conclusions that lead to refreshing existing campaigns or creating new ones. They can analyze raw consumer opinion at its source – this more likely to reveal the unvarnished truth, unlike the sometimes false positives often derived via focus groups and surveys.

Numerous firms offer superior software applications which make predictive analysis a relatively easy task – at least from a technical viewpoint.

8

Creativity and Intuition (or Posing the Right Question, at the Right Time, for the Right Data)

We have to continually be jumping off cliffs and developing our wings on the way down.

- Kurt Vonnegut -

"We live in the era of information and the trends that are hidden in the streams of data points," writes *TechNewsWorld's* Anjul Bhambhri. "Those who ask the right questions and apply the right technologies and talent are certain to crack the curious case of big data."

"Even if you have petabyes of data, you still need to know how to ask the right questions to apply it." So writes Alistair Croll, a founding partner at start-up accelerator Year One Labs and an analyst at Bitcurrent.

Croll cites the story of a friend, one which represents the classic example of a firm *not* asking the right questions with regard to Big Data: "He's a ridiculously heavy traveler, racking up hundreds of thousands of miles in the air each year. He's the kind of flier airlines dream of: loyal, well-heeled, and prone to last-minute, business-class trips. He's is exactly the kind of person an airline needs to court aggressively, one who represents a disproportionally large amount of revenues. He's an outlier of the best kind. He'd been a top-ranked passenger with United Airlines for nearly a decade, using their Mileage Plus program for everything from hotels to car rentals. And then his company was acquired. The acquiring firm had a contractual relationship with American Airlines, a competitor of United with a completely separate loyalty program. My friend's air travel on United and its partner airlines dropped to nearly nothing. He continued to book hotels in Shanghai, rent cars in Barcelona, and buy meals in Tahiti, and every one of those transactions was tied to his loyalty program with United. So the airline knew he was traveling – just not with them. Astonishingly, nobody ever called him to inquire about why he'd stopped flying with them. As a result, he's far less loyal than he was. But more importantly, United has lost a huge opportunity to try to win over a large company's business, with a passionate and motivated inside advocate."

Croll continues: "Ultimately, this is what my friend's airline example underscores. It takes an employee, deciding that the loss of high-value customers is important, to run a query of all their data and find him, and then turn that into a business advantage. Without the right questions, there really is no such thing as big data."

Per another commentator: "Apparently, business schools [are beginning to teach a skill generally] called 'data-based decision-making,' suggesting that the skill is reducible to pedagogical form. But 'asking the right question' remains more of an art than a science. It requires practice, patience, and time."

"Data analytics was once considered the purview of math, science and information-technology specialists," notes the *Wall Street Journal*. "Now barraged with data from the Web and other sources, companies want employees who can both sift through the information and help solve business problems or strategize. For example, luxury fashion company Elie Tahari Ltd. uses analytics to examine historical buying patterns and predict future clothing purchases. Northeastern pizza chain Papa Gino's Inc.

uses analytics to examine the use of its loyalty program and has succeeded in boosting the average customer's online order size. As the use of analytics grows quickly, companies will need employees who understand the data. A ... study from McKinsey & Co. found that by 2018, the U.S. will face a shortage of 1.5 million managers who can use data to shape business decisions."

But as Kevin Weil, Product Lead for Revenue at Twitter, put it during a recent talk, "asking the right question is hard." Which is the best explanation of why people like Kevin are so important. (As the head of the analytics team at Twitter, Weil is tasked with building distributed infrastructure and leveraging data analysis at a massive scale to help grow the popular micro-blogging service. With millions of monthly site visitors and many more interacting through API-based third party applications, Twitter has one of the world's most varied and interesting datasets.)

"The fact is that even when the boundaries of a dataset are narrowly defined ..., " writes Stephen O'Grady, cofounder of RedMonk, "it's easy to get lost in it. The trick is no longer merely being able to aggregate and operate on data; it's knowing what to do with it. Find the people that can do that, whether they're FTE's or consultants, and you'll have your competitive advantage. To [ask and] answer the right questions, you need the right people."

Simply put: "Big Data becomes Big Intelligence (otherwise known as Business Intelligence) only when put in the hands of the right people enabled to ask the right questions at the right time, on a huge scale. Anything else risks the information becoming redundant and the BI worthless before it's even discovered." So comments industry analyst Mike Pilcher. (Note that most practitioners also insist that, along with asking the right questions, it is important to eliminating bias, and correlation from causality.)

Weil is correct that asking the right question (or questions) is not easy.

Productivity guru Tony Robbins notes that thinking is a process of asking and answering questions. He stresses the importance of asking the *right* questions to get the *right* answers and therefore the *right* results. The wrong questions lead to useless answers and no results, at least no positive results.

Leadership guru Michael Hyatt, says the same thing in his own way: "Questions are powerful tools. They can ignite hope and lead to new insights. They can also destroy hope and keep us stuck in bad assumptions. The key is to be intentional and choose our questions well."

Perhaps the better phrase than *ask the right question* is *innovate the right question*. Innovation is key. Or, to resort to a cliche: be sure to *think outside the box*. (Einstein once said that if he only had an hour to solve a specific problem and his life depended on it, he'd devote the first 55 minutes to figuring out the right question to answer.)

Effective questioners look at an existing reality (data) from multiple (new) perspectives.

"Of course, it's not just a matter of being willing to question – it's also important to know how to question," writes Warren Berger (author of *CAD Monkeys, Dinosaur Babies, and T-Shaped People: Inside the World of Design Thinking*). "Innovation is driven by questions that are original, bold, counter-intuitive, and perceptive. ... Coming up with the right question, the one that casts a familiar challenge in a new light, is an art and science in itself. It demands that the questioner be able to look at an existing reality from multiple viewpoints, including, perhaps most importantly, that of the 'naive outsider.'"

Creative questioning is linked to the capacity to tolerate not knowing, to seek out paradoxes, to withstand the temptation of early closure, and to nurture the "courage of one's own stupidity" in questioning commonly accepted assumptions.

"You don't know what you don't know," says Bain consultant and partner Rasmus Wegener, "and if you don't know, it is hard to come up with the right question. You need to be well-versed in both the business and the data." Then you have to begin to bravely ask *why* and *what*.

Why are our digital subscription renewals down 10% in Boston, but booming everywhere else, and what available data can we merge and sort creatively in order to move toward an answer? What customer-appreciation program enhancements will best serve our purpose of improving user retention, and how can we leverage customer-appreciation-points usage data to infer an answer? What trends can we expect to see in vis-a-vis bandwidth usage on our network come Superbowl Sunday? (What spike did we see last year on the same day? What percentages of the spike represented cell phones, tablets, PCs? How have the hardware demographics of our users changed in the past 365 days. And what is the most efficient, logical way to correlate this data and infer an answer?)

In sum: Move forward bravely – but rationally – into the unknown. Think on your feet. Realize fully what data is at your fingertips. Think analytically and creatively about how to leverage that combined data to learn and predict. Reach for knowledge. Go for it.

My greatest strength as a consultant is to be ignorant and ask a few questions.

- Peter Drucker

9

Data Visualization (or Telling the Story)

A picture is worth a thousand words.

"If you're trying to extract useful information from an ever-increasing inflow of data, you'll likely find *visualization* useful – whether it's to show patterns or trends with graphics instead of mountains of text, or to try to explain complex issues to a nontechnical audience." So writes *InfoWorld's* Sharon Machlis.

Rebeckah Blewett, product manager for Dundas Data Visualization Inc., explains: "The practice of representing information visually is nothing new. Scientists, students, and analysts have been using data visualization for centuries to track everything from astrological phenomena to stock prices." Data visualization, when done correctly, is a highly effective way to analyze large amounts of data to identify correlations, trends, outliers, patterns, and business conditions.

Many of us have experienced rudimentary forms of data visualization in our day-to-day experience of the Web. The popular TwitterEarth, for example, shows real-time tweets from all over the world on a 3D globe. It's a great visualization tool to see where tweets are coming from in real time and discover new people to follow. It's also fascinating just to sit and watch. Another simple example is the Flickr Related Tag Browser, which allows you to search for a series of tags and see related tags. Clicking on a different tag brings up new related tags. You can zoom into the tag selected in the center of the screen by hovering and see images tagged with that word. It also gives a total image count and lets you browse by page. And another is TED Sphere, which shows videos from the TED conference in a spherical format with 3D navigation. You can view the sphere from inside or outside and the layout of videos is based on semantic compatibility.

Data presentation can be beautiful, elegant and descriptive," writes Vitaly Freidman of *Smashing Magazine*. "There is a variety of conventional ways to visualize data -tables, histograms, pie charts and bar graphs are being used every day, in every project and on every possible occasion. However, to convey a message ... effectively, sometimes you need more than just a simple pie chart of your results. In fact, there are much better, profound, creative and absolutely fascinating ways to visualize data. Many of them might become ubiquitous in the next few years."

In essence, the task of data visualization involves creating data layers and presenting these as easy-to-comprehend graphics for viewing by data analysts and non-tech decision-makers. Think of it as the graphical blending of data.

"Graph-based visual analysis is a highly effective method for capturing and understanding relationships between data that are not quantitative in nature," writes industry pundit Jin H. Kim. "This method and technology has been used in diverse fields such as intelligence and law enforcement to customer sentiment and network topology analysis to uncover hidden insights in growing data that was not possible when relying only on traditional analytics."

Kim continues: "The combination of rich data collection, advanced analytics operating across both structured and unstructured data, and efficiently storing and analyzing information in quantities unimagined just a few years back, have created a new era of data analysis in general and visual analysis in particular. We can now look at the networks representing relationships between data as not just static topologies, but rather as 'dynamic networks' with their own behavioral pattern in terms of change, sequence of change, and uncertainties of change, combined with the ability to integrate information from complex event processing engines and other 'event driven' information sources. These new developments promise to bring about a new dawn of information use, enabling smarter, timelier decision-making in various fields of human endeavor."

As suggested previously (ala Twitter), data visualization plays a key role in real-time structured network analysis (SNA) – the modeling of relationships and overlaps between disparate groups of people.

"Social network analysis uses graph theoretic ideas and applies them with the premise that the structure of the graph can be used to understand and identify critical relationships and influential people. ... " writes Elizabeth Hefner of Tom Sawyer Software. " Recent advancements in network analysis involving complex network topologies with multiple relationships between nodes, network behavior that is based on uncertain information, and time-based change of networks, have enhanced the value of incorporating advanced network analysis techniques as a key part of an analytics tool-set to aid in better understanding data relationships. More organizations are beginning to understand that with advanced visual analysis technology, they can build integrated insights across all of their available data, enabling them to better understand emerging opportunities and threats. ... The combination of advanced visualization techniques, together with social network analysis techniques, will help bridge the emerging gap between the vast amounts of available information in Big Data and the available resources to better understand them."

Numerous firms provide quite elegant, effective and powerful tools for data visualization.

These are just two options among many.

Edward Tufte – author of the classic *Visual Display of Quantitative Information* – has written: "The commonality between science and art is in trying to see profoundly – to develop strategies of seeing and showing." No truer words.

10

Cassandra

There's a way to do it better – find it.

- Thomas Edison -

Time to meet the Apache Cassandra NoSQL open-source distributed database management system. Cassandra is an absolutely essential tool for data scientists. There is virtually no company today concerned with large, active data sets which does not use Cassandra. The short list? Netflix, Twitter, Reddit, Cisco, OpenX, Digg, CloudKick, and Ooyala.

Cassandra offers all-important linear scalability and reliable fault-tolerance – the two key attributes of any platform required to manage mission-critical data. Per Apache: The platform offers optimal support for replicating across multiple data-centers; in this it allows lower latency and protection against regional outages. In short, Cassandra is a brilliantly efficient, non-traditional database that's been designted to easily scale up to massive data sets.

This free distribution from the Apache Software Foundation offers column indexes, log-structured updates, support for materialized views, and elegant built-in caching.

The database is completely fault tolerant. Cassandra automatically replicates (backs-up) data to multiple nodes or, if you prefer, to multiple data centers. Failing nodes can be replaced with absolutely no downtime interruption. This is, of course, a decentralized platform. Every node in a cluster is identical. There are no network bottlenecks, and no single points of failure.

At the same time, Cassandra is elastic. When new machines are added, read and write throughput increase linearly. There's no downtime, no interruption.

As of Release 1.0 in October of 2011, the system's interface has been greatly simplified from that of previous beta releases. "We're consciously signaling that Cassandra is ready for mere mortals," said Jonathan Ellis, who is Apache's vice president in charge of the Cassandra project, jokingly referring to the amount administrative expertise needed to deploy previous versions of the software. "Dealing with very large amounts of data in real-time is a must for most businesses today. Cassandra accommodates high query volumes, provides enterprise-grade reliability, and scales easily to meet future growth requirements -while using fewer resources than traditional solutions."

Ellis says the difference between traditional databases like MySQL and Cassandra is the difference between analytic big data and real-time big data. He further notes that Hadoop itself is strictly an analytical system rather than a real time or transaction oriented system (ala Cassandra). Ellis: "On the real-time side, Cassandra's strongest competitors are probably Riak and HBase. Riak is backed by Basho, and I believe Cloudera supports HBase although it's not their focus. For analytics, everyone is standardizing on Hadoop, and there are a number of companies pushing that. ... "

Users find Cassandra indispensable.

"As the most-widely deployed mobile rich media advertising platform, Medialets uses Apache Cassandra for handling time series based logging from our production operations infrastructure," says Joe Stein, Chief Architect of Medialets. "We store contiguous counts for data points for each second, minute, hour, day, month so we can review trends over time as well as the current real time set of information for tens of thousands of data points. Cassandra makes it possible for us to manage this intensive data set ... "

Matthew Conway, CTO of Backupify notes: "Apache Cassandra makes it possible for us to build a business around really high write loads in a scalable fashion without having to build and operate our own sharing layer. The [latest] release of Cassandra ... is an exciting milestone for the project and we look forward to exploring the new features and performance enhancements."

11

Academic Programs

I have never let my schooling interfere with my education.

\- Mark Twain -

"Prediction: in the next 10 years we will see the majority of major universities start masters degree programs, or Ph.D. programs, in data science, data analytics, business analytics, or the like." So wrote Cathy O'Neil on her *Mathbabe* blog in January of 2012. "They will exist somewhere in the intersection of the fields of statistics, operations research, and computer science, and business. They will teach students how to use machine learning algorithms and various statistical methods, and how to design expert systems. Then they will send these newly minted data scientists out to work at McKinsey, Google, Yahoo, and possibly Data Without Borders."

But, adds O'Neil, there are serious aspects of such programs yet to be sorted out. "Relevance: will they also teach the underlying theory well enough so that the students will know when the techniques are applicable? Skepticism: will they in general teach enough about robustness in order for the emerging data scientists to be sufficiently skeptical of the resulting models? Ethics: will they incorporate understanding the impact of the models so that students will think to understand the ethical implications of modeling? Will they have a well-developed notion of the Modeler's Hippocratic Oath by then? Open modeling: will they focus narrowly on making businesses more efficient or will they focus on developing platforms which are open to the public and allow people more views into the models, especially when the models in question affect that public?"

A few such programs already exist.

Consider, for example, the Institute for Advanced Analytics at North Carolina State University. Per a recent release from this institution: "Record high salary offers have earned the Master of Science in Analytics (MSA) Class of 2012 the distinction of being the most sought-after MSA cohort since the Institute's inception in 2007. Thirty-eight candidates seeking employment logged a record-breaking 591 initial job interviews with 54 employers during the placement period that started in January – an average of 15 interviews per student. Ninety-seven percent of the Class of 2012 received one or more offers of employment, and most have already accepted their new positions. This marks the fifth straight year the Institute will place over 90-percent of its graduates by commencement despite hard economic times. The average base salary offer registered an increase of 10-percent to $89,300. Over 79-percent of the students had 2 or more job offers; 47-percent had 3 or more. Seven candidates had 4 or more job offers, and the maximum number of offers was 7. The Institute hosted or otherwise played a role in arranging 99-percent of the interviews conducted. Twenty-three employers made offers of employment; sixteen employers tendered offers to more than one student. Employers represent a cross-section of industry, including: banking and financial services, consulting, energy, gaming, healthcare, Internet, pharmaceuticals, research and software. Employer types range from new ventures to large multinational companies, and the types of jobs range from entry level analysts to managerial and executive level positions. Salary offers for graduates set an all-time high for the program. The average base salary offer

for MSA candidates with professional experience
(half the class) is $99,600, an increase of $11,100 over
last year. Offers range from $65,000 to $160,000 for
candidates with experience. The average base salary
offer for candidates without prior work experience is
$76,400, up $3,100 from last year. Offers range from
$60,000 to $100,000 for candidates with no prior
professional work experience."

In March of 2012, Syracuse University's School of
Information Studies (iSchool) announced a new
graduate certificate program in data science.

According to iSchool Dean Elizabeth D. Liddy:
"The iSchool is helping lead the dialogue in defining
data science within the academic community and for
our partner organizations. In doing so, students in
this program have the rare opportunity to have an
impact on the first wave of data science in a wide
range of organizations. This will help institutions and
affiliates clarify the murky definitions of data science
as it infiltrates public consciousness over the next five
to 10 years. While predictive analysis is not new, the
ability to apply this practice to large data sets,
whether structured or unstructured, is an
evolutionary leap forward for the world.
Additionally, the iSchool's focus on connecting people
and ideas through technology keeps graduates poised

to not only work in data science but to have the perspective needed to help it grow from its infancy."

Susan A. Dischiave, assistant professor of practice at the iSchool, describes the iSchool as a superior place for teaching this field of information expertise. She cites the school's information and data orientation, expertise in natural language processing and faculty who deal in data mining, social media, and structured and unstructured data fields. "We're just a perfect fit to help organizations handle these problems and to help students prepare to go into the workforce. Organizations are going to need to get their arms around the growing levels of structured operational data as well as enormous amounts of unstructured data that's flowing from other areas; it's a big problem, and it's very challenging."

Another outstanding resource is Rensselaer Polytechnic's Data Science Research Center. Per DSRC literature: "The objective of DSRC is to become a center with national and international visibility, and provide support and infrastructure to its members for solving data centric and data intensive research problems by capitalizing on Rensselaer's super computer center (CCNI) and experimental media and performing arts center (EMPAC). Members of DSRC will collaborate and interact via workshops in specific topics, group meetings, seminars, student internships at industrial research labs. DSRC will offer an educational and training program for graduate students and post-docs to prepare the next generation data scientist and engineers."

Numerous other superior programs exist, with many more in development.

New technology is common, new thinking is rare.

- *Sir Peter Blake*

About the Authors

Noreen Burlingame is a leading IT consultant. Her publications include New Street's *The Little Book of BIG DATA, 2012 Edition.* Lars Nielsen's bestsellers include *The Little Book of Cloud Computing* and *Computing: A Business History.*

About the Publisher

Founded June of 2010, New Street Communications, LLC publishes first-quality nonfiction in a range of fields (also, through Dark Hall Press, first-quality original horror and science fiction). New Street's nonfiction interests include the intersection of digital technology and society; transformative business communication and innovation (particularly the conceptualizing of elegant new tools, markets, products and paradigms); environmental issues; socially-relevant children's literature; travel; and literary criticism. We are located in the historic seaport town of Wickford, RI, near Newport.

newstreetcommunications.com

Also from New Street ...

Computing: A Business History by Lars Nielsen

The Little Book of Cloud Computing by Lars Nielsen

The Little Book of Scientific Writing by Nancy Fox

and more ...

15479566R00040

Made in the USA
Charleston, SC
05 November 2012